mommy

mamá

daddy

papi

boy

niño

girl

niña

1

one

uno

2

two

dos

3

three

tres

4

four

cuatro

5

five

cinco

6

six

seis

7

seven

siete

8

eight

ocho

9

nine

nueve

10

ten

diez

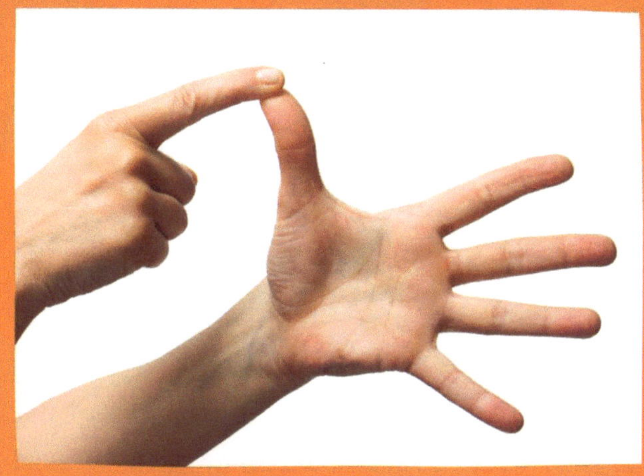

count

contar

write

escribir

draw

dibujar

paint

pintar

circle

círculo

square

cuadrado

rectangle

rectángulo

triangle

triángulo

star

estrella

black

negro

white

blanco

brown

marrón

red

rojo

blue

azul

yellow

amarillo

green

verde

purple

morado

gray

gris

orange

naranja

pink

rosa

apple

manzana

banana

plátano

pineapple

piña

watermelon

sandía

pear

pera

grapes

uvas

mango

mango

peach

melocotón

strawberry

fresa

cherry

cereza

orange

naranja

coconut

coco

lemon

limón

mushroom

seta

corn

maíz

tomato

tomate

pumpkin

calabaza

cucumber

pepino

carrot

zanahoria

potato

patata

zucchini

calabacín

spinach

espinacas

cauliflower

coliflor

egg

huevo

plate

plato

spoon

cuchara

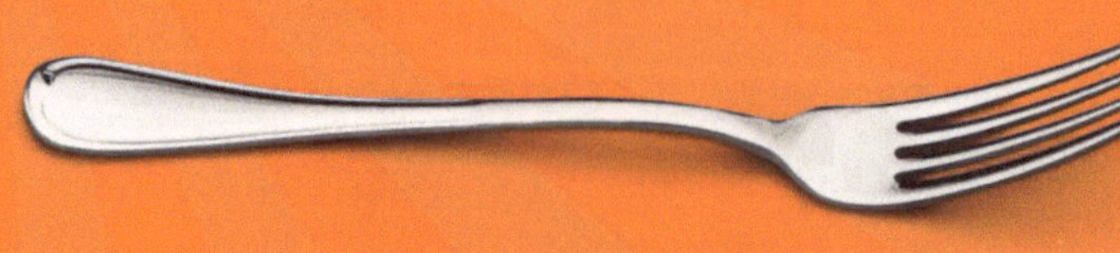

knife

cuchillo

fork

tenedor

cake

pastel

baby bottle

biberón

candies

caramelos

cheese

queso

drink

beber

eat

comer

hot

caliente

cold

frío

small

pequeño

big

grande

 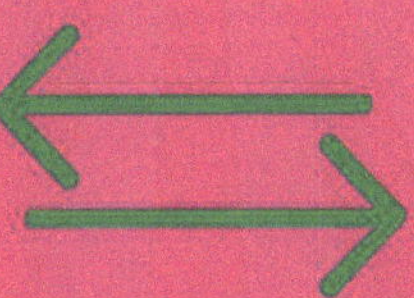

short

corto

long

largo

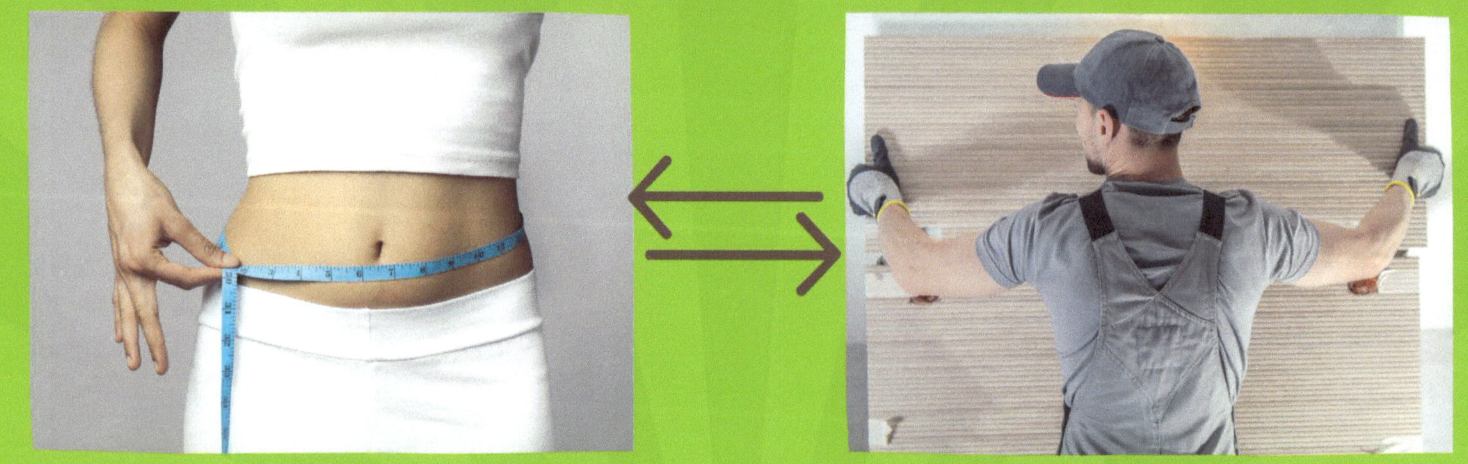

thin

delgado

large

grande

easy

fácil

difficult

difícil

stand up

levantarse

sit down

sentarse

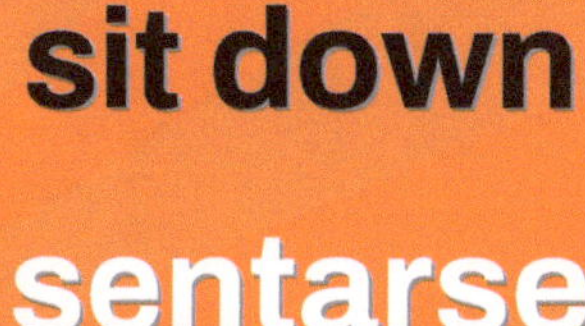

sweet

dulce

salty

salado

heavy

pesado

light

ligero

in

en

out

fuera

dirty

sucio

clean

limpio

close

cerrado

open

abierto

pencils

lápices

clock

reloj

key

llave

book

libro

bed

cama

crib

cuna

table

mesa

chair

silla

car

coche

bike

bicicleta

plane

avión

boat

barco

train

tren

helicopter

helicóptero

firetruck

camión de bomberos

firefighter

bombero

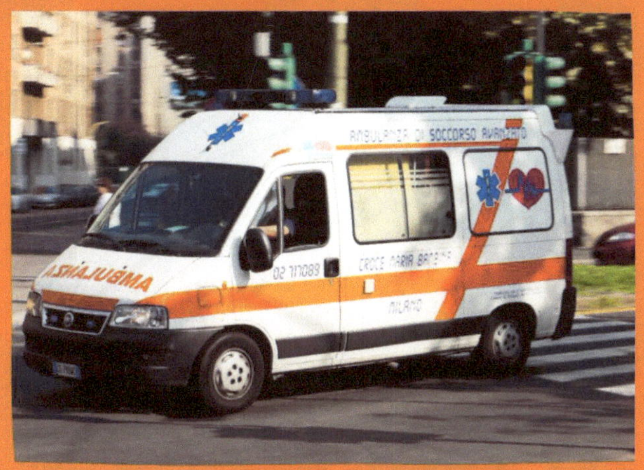

ambulance

ambulancia

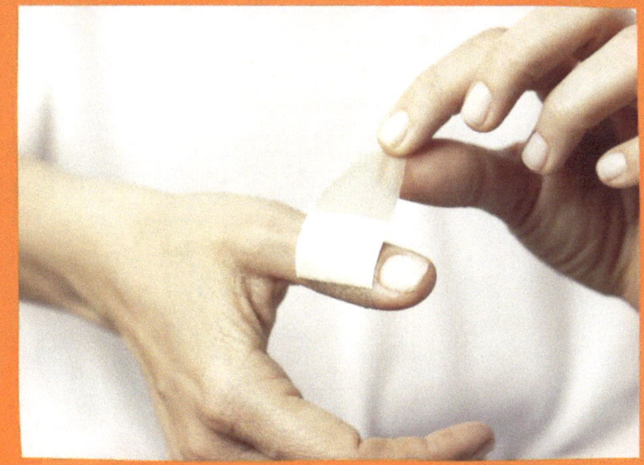

bandage

vendaje

paramedic

paramédico

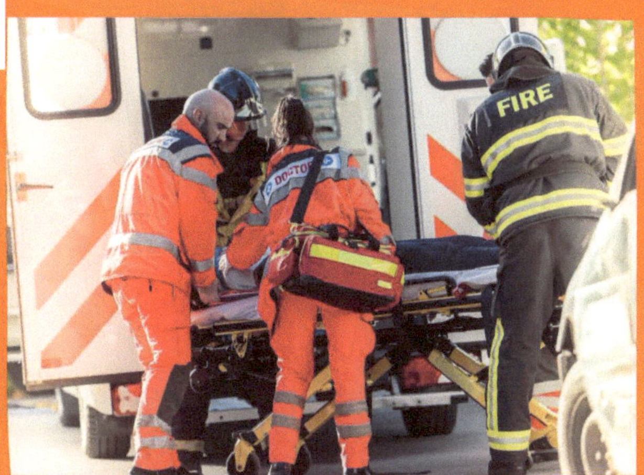

rescue team

equipo de rescate

forest

bosque

mountain

montaña

grass

hierba

sand

arena

tree

árbol

flower

flor

butterfly

mariposa

ant

hormiga

cat

gato

dog

perro

horse

caballo

mouse

ratón

cow

vaca

pig

cerdo

sheep

oveja

duck

pato

goose

ganso

rabbit

conejo

fish

pez

vet

veterinario

doctor

doctor

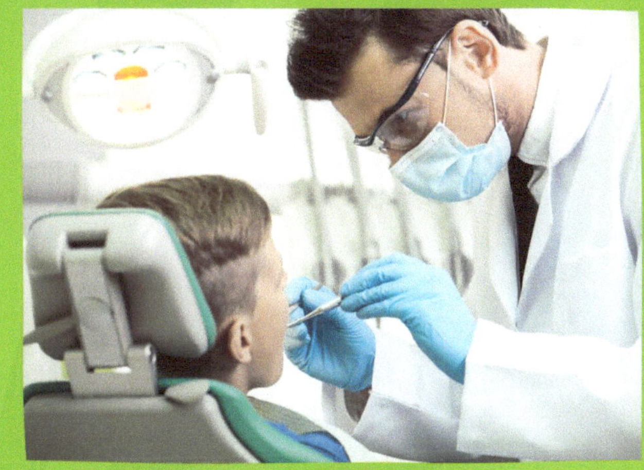

dentist

dentista

pharmacist

farmacéutico

nurse

enfermera

head

cabeza

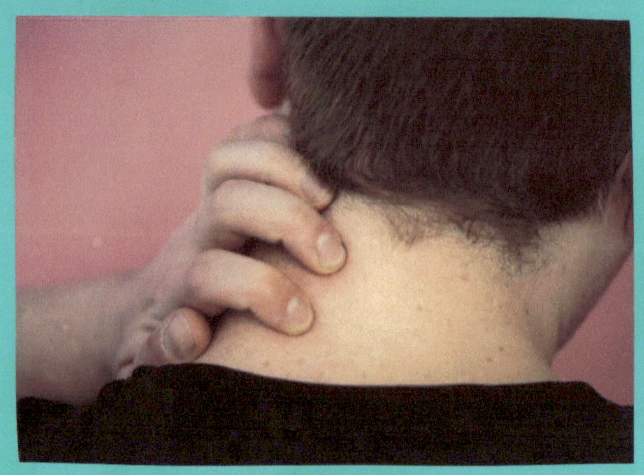

neck

cuello

foot

pie

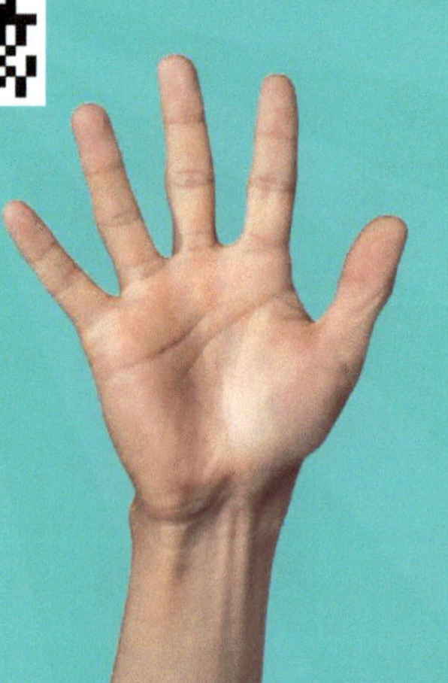

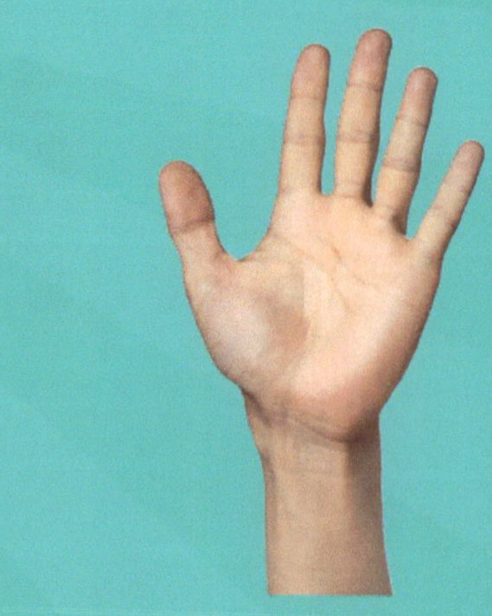

hand

mano

teeth

dientes

eye

ojo

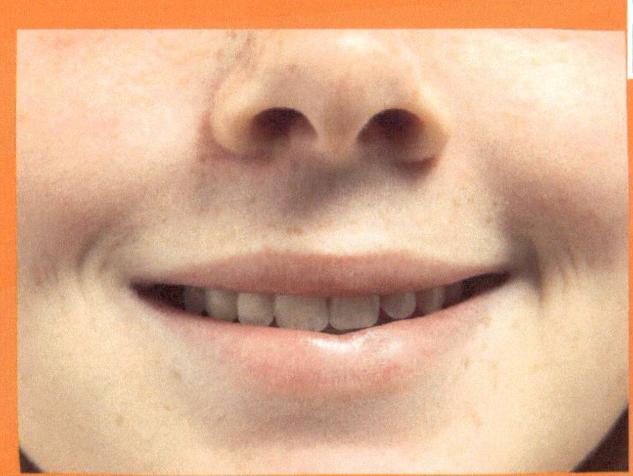

mouth

boca

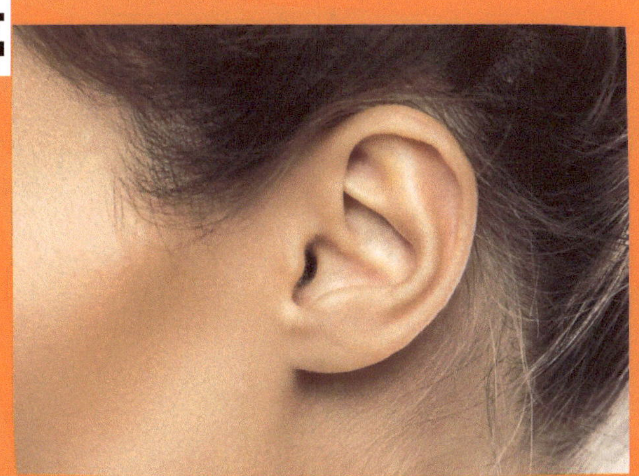

ear

oreja

hat

sombrero

dress

vestido

pants

pantalones

shoes

zapatos

coat

abrigo

scarf

bufanda

umbrella

paraguas

glasses

gafas

sun

sol

cloudy

nublado

rainy

lluvioso

moon

luna